The Poetry Of Francis Ledwidge

Francis Edward Ledwidge was born on 19th August, 1887 in the small village of Janeville in Slane, Co Meath in Ireland to parents that believed strongly in education. However at the age of 5 his father died and the entire family, already desperately poor, was forced into work and by 13 this entailed whatever job was to hand - from farm hand to road labourer. Throughout this time he applied himself to his poetry writing whenever and wherever he could. His work was published on a regular basis from the age of 14 in the Drogheda Independent, his local paper.

Francis was an ardent Nationalist and was well known for his Sinn Fein and trade union activism. This association got him fired from his job at the Slane copper mines, for organising a strike for better working conditions, but prompted his appointment as the Secretary to the Slane branch of the Meath Labour Union. Francis found patronage from Lord Dunsany who was well known in literary circles and despite the Lord's offer of regular funds if he did not fight in World War I. Francis was originally opposed to the War (he had helped to found the Irish Volunteers a short time before) but then changed his view and enlisted and fought for Lord Dunsany's regiment, part of the 10th Irish Division. He thrived in the army finding promotion, happy to be serving Ireland and continuing to write but on 31st July 1917 his body was blown to bits by a shell explosion.

Francis Ledwidge, the patriot and nationalist has been dubbed the soldier poet or peasant poet and whilst his work has been recognised for its vivid descriptions and intense brilliance, it has been sorely neglected.

GW00750801

Index Of Poems

A Soldier's Grave
Then in the lull of midnight, gentle arms
Lifted him slowly down the slopes of death
Lest he should hear again the mad alarms
Of battle, dying moans, and painful breath.

And where the earth was soft for flowers we made
A grave for him that he might better rest.
So, Spring shall come and leave it seet arrayed,
And there the lark shall turn her dewy nest

At A Poet's Grave
When I leave down this pipe my friend
And sleep with flowers I loved, apart,
My songs shall rise in wilding things
Whose roots are in my heart.

And here where that sweet poet sleeps
I hear the songs he left unsung,
When winds are fluttering the flowers
And summer-bells are rung.

Lament For The Poets: 1916
I heard the Poor Old Woman say:
"At break of day the fowler came,
And took my blackbirds from their songs

Who loved me well thro' shame and blame

No more from lovely distances
Their songs shall bless me mile by mile,
Nor to white Ashbourne call me down
To wear my crown another while.

With bended flowers the angels mark
For the skylark the place they lie,
From there its little family
Shall dip their wings first in the sky.

And when the first suprise of flight
Sweet songs excite, from the far dawn
Shall there come blackbirds loud with love,
Sweet echoesmof the singers gone.

But in the lovely hush of eve
Weeping I grieve the silent bills"
I heard the Poor Old Woman say
In Derry of the little hills.

Lament For Thomas McDonagh
He shall not hear the bittern cry
In the wild sky, where he is lain,
Nor voices of the sweeter birds,
Above the wailing of the rain.

Nor shall he know when loud March blows
Thro' slanting snows her fanfare shrill,
Blowing to flame the golden cup
Of many an upset daffodil.

But when the Dark Cow leaves the moor
And pastures poor with greedy weeds
Perhaps he'll hear her low at morn
Lifting her horn in pleasant meads.

To One Dead
A blackbird singing
On a moss-upholstered stone,
Bluebells swinging,
Shadows wildly blown,

A song in the wood,
A ship on the sea.
The song was for you
and the ship was for me.

A blackbird singing
I hear in my troubled mind,
Bluebells swinging,
I see in a distant wind.
But sorrow and silence,
Are the wood's threnody,
The silence for you
and the sorrow for me.

Soliloquy
When I was young I had a care
Lest I should cheat me of my share
Of that which makes it sweet to strive
For life, and dying still survive,
A name in sunshine written higher
Than lark or poet dare aspire.

But I grew weary doing well.
Besides, 'twas sweeter in that hell,
Down with the loud banditti people
Who robbed the orchards, climbed the steeple
For jackdaws' eyes and made the cock
Crow ere 'twas daylight on the clock.
I was so very bad the neighbours
Spoke of me at their daily labours.

And now I'm drinking wine in France,
The helpless child of circumstance.
To-morrow will be loud with war,
How will I be accounted for?

It is too late now to retrieve
A fallen dream, too late to grieve
A name unmade, but not too late
To thank the gods for what is great;
A keen-edged sword, a soldier's heart,
Is greater than a poet's art.
And greater than a poet's fame
A little grave that has no name.

To One Who Comes Now And Then

When you come in, it seems a brighter fire
Crackles upon the hearth invitingly,
The household routine which was wont to tire ,
Grows full of novelty.

You sit upon our home-upholstered chair
And talk of matters wonderful and strange,
Of books, and travel, customs old which dare
The gods of Time and Change.

Till we with inner word our care refute
Laughing that this our bosoms yet assails,
While there are maidens dancing to a flute
In Andalusian vales.

And sometimes from my shelf of poems you take
And secret meanings to our hearts disclose,
As when the winds of June the mid bush shake
We see the hidden rose.

And when the shadows muster, and each tree
A moment flutters, full of shutting wings,
You take the fiddle and mysteriously
Wake wonders on the strings.

And in my garden, grey with misty flowers,
Low echoes fainter than a beetle's horn
Fill all the corners with it, like sweet showers
Of bells, in the owl's morn.

Come often, friend, with welcome and surprise
We'll greet you from the sea or from the town;
Come when you like and from whatever skies
Above you smile or frown.

A Fairy Hunt

Who would hear the fairy horn
Calling all the hounds of Finn
Must be in a lark's nest born
When the moon is very thin.

I who have the gift can hear

Hounds and horn and tally ho,
And the tongue of Bran as clear
As Christmas bells across the snow.

And beside my secret place
Hurries by the fairy fox,
With the moonrise on his face,
Up and down the mossy rocks.

Then the music of a horn
And the flash of scarlet men,
Thick as poppies in the corn
All across the dusky glen.

Oh! the mad delight of chase!
Oh ! the shouting and the cheer !
Many an owl doth leave his place
In the dusty tree to hear.

Two Songs

I will come no more awhile,
Song-time is over.
A fire is burning in my heart,
I was ever a rover.

You will hear me no more awhile,
The birds are dumb,
And a voice in the distance calls
'Come,' and ' Come.'

At Currabwee

Every night at Currabwee
Little men with leather hats
Mend the boots of Faery
From the tough wings of the bats.
So my mother told to me,
And she is wise you will agree.

Louder than a cricket's wing
All night long their hammer's glee
Times the merry songs they sing
Of Ireland glorious and free.
So I heard Joseph Plunkett say,

You know he heard them but last May.

And when the night is very cold
They warm their hands against the light
Of stars that make the waters gold
Where they are labouring all the night.
So Pearse said, and he knew the truth,
Among the stars he spent his youth.

And I, myself, have often heard
Their singing as the stars went by,
For am I not of those who reared
The banner of old Ireland high,
From Dublin town to Turkey's shores,
And where the Vardar loudly roars?

Una Bawn
Una Bawn, the days are long,
And the seas I cross are wide,
I must go when Ireland needs,
And you must bide.

And should I not return to you
When the sails are on the tide,
'Tis you will find the days so long,
Una Bawn, and I must bide.

Pan
He knows the safe ways and unsafe
And he will lead the lambs to fold,
Gathering them with his merry pipe,
The gentle and the overbold.

He counts them over one by one,
And leads them back by cliff and steep,
To grassy hills where dawn is wide,
And they may run and skip and leap.

And just because he loves the lambs
He settles them for rest at noon,
And plays them on his oaten pipe
The very wonder of a tune.

Dawn

Quiet miles of golden sky,
And in my heart a sudden flower.
I want to clap my hands and cry
For Beauty in her secret bower.

Quiet golden miles of dawn
Smiling all the East along;
And in my heart nigh fully blown,
A little rose-bud of a song.

My Mother

God made my mother on an April day,
From sorrow and the mist along the sea,
Lost birds' and wanderers' songs and ocean spray,
And the moon loved her wandering jealously.

Beside the ocean's din she combed her hair,
Singing the nocturne of the passing ships,
Before her earthly lover found her there
And kissed away the music from her lips.

She came unto the hills and saw the change
That brings the swallow and the geese in turns.
But there was not a grief she deeméd strange,
For there is that in her which always mourns.

Kind heart she has for all on hill or wave
Whose hopes grew wings like ants to fly away.
I bless the God Who such a mother gave
This poor bird-hearted singer of a day.

Thoughts At The Trysting Stile

Come, May, and hang a white flag on each thorn,
Make truce with earth and heaven; the April child
Now hides her sulky face deep in the morn
Of your new flowers by the water wild
And in the ripples of the rising grass,
And rushes bent to let the south wind pass
On with her tumult of swift nomad wings,
And broken domes of downy dandelion.

Only in spasms now the blackbird sings.
The hour is all a-dream.

Nets of woodbine
Throw woven shadows over dreaming flowers,
And dreaming, a bee-luring lily bends
Its tender bell where blue dyke-water cowers
Thro' briars and folded ferns, and gripping ends
Of wild convolvulus.

The lark's sky-way
Is desolate.
I watch an apple-spray
Beckon across a wall as if it knew
I wait the calling of the orchard maid.
Inly I fell she will come in blue,
With yellow on her hair, and two curls strayed
Out of her comb's loose stocks, and I shall steal
Behind and lay my hands upon her eyes,
'Look not, but be my Psyche! '

And her peal
Of laughter will ring far, and as she tries
For freedom I will call her names of flowers
That climb up walls; then thro' the twilight hours
We'll talk about the loves of ancient queens,
And kisses like wasp-honey, false and sweet,
And how we are entangled in love's snares
Like wind-looped flowers.

Behind The Closed Eye
I walk the old frequented ways
That wind around the tangled braes,
I live again the sunny days
Ere I the city knew.

And scenes of old again are born,
The woodbine lassoing the thorn,
And drooping Ruth-like in the corn
The poppies weep the dew.

Above me in their hundred schools
The magpies bend their young to rules,
And like an apron full of jewels
The dewy cobweb swings.

And frisking in the stream below
The troutlets make the circles flow,
And the hungry crane doth watch them grow
As a smoker does his rings.

Above me smokes the little town,
With its whitewashed walls and roofs of brown
And its octagon spire toned smoothly down
As the holy minds within.

And wondrous impudently sweet,
Half of him passion, half conceit,
The blackbird calls adown the street
Like the piper of Hamelin.

I hear him, and I feel the lure
Drawing me back to the homely moor,
I'll go and close the mountain's door
On the city's strife and din.

To A Sparrow
Because you have no fear to mingle
Wings with those of greater part,
So like me, with song I single
Your sweet impudence of heart.

And when prouder feathers go where
Summer holds her leafy show,
You still come to us from nowhere
Like grey leaves across the snow.

In back ways where odd and end go
To your meals you drop down sure,
Knowing every broken window
Of the hospitable poor.

There is no bird half so harmless,
None so sweetly rude as you,
None so common and so charmless,
None of virtues nude as you.

But for all your faults I love you,
For you linger with us still,

Though the wintry winds reprove you
And the snow is on the hill.

Fairies
Maiden-poet, come with me
To the heaped up cairn of Maeve,
And there we'll dance a fairy dance
Upon a fairy's grave.

In and out among the trees,
Filling all the night with sound,
The morning, strung upon her star,
Shall chase us round and round.

What are we but fairies too,
Living but in dreams alone,
Or, at the most, but children still,
Innocent and overgrown ?

To An Old Quill Of Lord Dunsany's
Before you leave my hands' abuses
To lie where many odd things meet you,
Neglected darkling of the Muses,
I, the last of singers, greet you.

Snug in some white wing they found you,
On the Common bleak and muddy,
Noisy goslings gobbling round you.
In the pools of sunset, ruddy.

Have you sighed in wings untravelled
For the heights where others view the
Bluer widths of heaven, and marvelled
At the utmost top of Beauty?

No ! it cannot be ; the soul you
Sigh with craves nor begs of us.
From such heights a poet stole you
From a wing of Pegasus.

You have been where gods were sleeping
In the dawn of new creations,
Ere they woke to woman's weeping

At the broken thrones of nations.

You have seen this old world shattered
By old gods it disappointed,
Lying up in darkness, battered
By wild comets, unanointed.

But for Beauty unmolested
Have you still the sighing olden ?
I know mountains heather-crested,
Waters white, and waters golden.

There I'd keep you, in the lowly
Beauty-haunts of bird and poet,
Sailing in a wing, the holy
Silences of lakes below it.

But I leave you by where no man
Finds you, when I too be gone
From the puddles on this common
Over the dark Rubicon.

Old Clo
I was just coming in from the garden,
Or about to go fishing for eels,
And, smiling, I asked you to pardon
My boots very low at the heels.
And I thought that you never would go,
As you stood in the doorway ajar,
For my heart would keep saying, 'Old Clo',
You're found out at last as you are.'

I was almost ashamed to acknowledge
That I was the quarry you sought,
For was I not bred in a college
And reared in a mansion, you thought.
And now in the latest style cut
With fortune more kinder I go
To welcome you half-ways. Ah (but
I was nearer the gods when ' Old Clo'.'

The Wife Of Llew

And Gwydion said to Math, when it was Spring:
"Come now and let us make a wife for Llew."
And so they broke broad boughs yet moist with dew,
And in a shadow made a magic ring:
They took the violet and the meadow-sweet
To form her pretty face, and for her feet
They built a mound of daisies on a wing,
And for her voice they made a linnet sing
In the wide poppy blowing for her mouth.
And over all they chanted twenty hours.
And Llew came singing from the azure south
And bore away his wife of birds and flowers.

Ceol Sidhe

When May is here, and every morn
Is dappled with pied bells,
And dewdrops glance along the thorn
And wings flash in the dells,
I take my pipe and play a tune
Of dreams, a whispered melody,
For feet that dance beneath the moon
In fairy jollity.

And when the pastoral hills are grey
And the dim stars are spread,
A scamper fills the grass like play
Of feet where fairies tread.
And many a little whispering thing
Is calling the Shee.
The dewy bells of evening ring,
And all is melody.

Had I A Golden Pound (After The Irish)

Had I a golden pound to spend,
My love should mend and sew no more.
And I would buy her a little quern,
Easy to turn on the kitchen floor.

And for her windows curtains white,
With birds in flight and flowers in bloom,
To face with pride the road to town,
And mellow down her sunlit room.

And with the silver change we'd prove
The truth of Love to life's own end,
With hearts the years could but embolden,
Had I a golden pound to spend.

The Sylph

I saw you and I named a flower
That lights with blue a woodland space,
I named a bird of the red hour
And a hidden fairy place.

And then I saw you not, and knew
Dead leaves were whirling down the mist,
And something lost was crying through -
An evening of amethyst.

In France

The silence of maternal hills
Is round me in my evening dreams;
And round me music-making rills
And mingling waves of pastoral streams.

Whatever way I turn I find
The path is old unto me still.
The hills of home are in my mind,
And there I wander as I will.

A Little Boy In The Morning

He will not come, and still I wait.
He whistles at another gate
Where angels listen. Ah I know
He will not come, yet if I go
How shall I know he did not pass
barefooted in the flowery grass?

The moon leans on one silver horn
Above the silhouettes of morn,
And from their nest-sills finches whistle
Or stooping pluck the downy thistle.
How is the morn so gay and fair
Without his whistling in its air?

The world is calling, I must go.
How shall I know he did not pass
Barefooted in the shining grass?

Ireland
I called you by sweet names by wood and linn,
You answered not because my voice was new,
And you were listening for the hounds of Finn
And the long hosts of Lugh.

And so, I came unto a windy height
And cried my sorrow, but you heard no wind,
For you were listening to small ships in flight,
And the wail on hills behind.

And then I left you, wandering the war
Armed with will, from distant goal to goal,
To find you at the last free as of yore,
Or die to save your soul.

And then you called to us from far and near
To bring your crown from out the deeps of time,
It is my grief your voice I couldn't hear
In such a distant clime.

The Find
I took a reed and blew a tune,
And sweet it was and very clear
To be about a little thing
That only few hold dear.

Three times the cuckoo named himself,
But nothing heard him on the hill,
Where I was piping like an elf
The air was very still.

'Twas all about a little thing
I made a mystery of sound,
I found it in a fairy ring
Upon a fairy mound.

The Rushes

The rushes nod by the river
As the winds on the loud waves go,
And the things they nod of are many,
For it's many the secret they know.

And I think they are wise as the fairies
Who lived ere the hills were high,
They nod so grave by the river
To everyone passing by.

If they would tell me their secrets
[: I would go by a hidden way,
To the rath when the moon retiring
Dips dim horns into the gray.

And a fairy-girl out of Leinster
In a long dance I should meet,
My heart to her heart beating,
My feet in rhyme with her feet.

Lady Fair

Lady fair, have we not met
In our lives elsewhere?
Darkling in my mind to-night
Faint fair faces dare
Memory's old unfaithfulness
To what was true and fair.
Long of memory is Regret,
But what Regret has taken flight
Through my memory's silences?
Lo ! I turn it to the light.
'Twas but a pleasure in distress,
Too faint and far off for redress.
But some light glancing in your hair
And in the liquid of your eyes
Seem to murmur old good-byes
In our lives elsewhere.
Have we not met. Lady fair?

The Shadow People

Old lame Bridget doesn't hear
Fairy music in the grass
When the gloaming's on the mere

And the shadow people pass:
Never hears their slow grey feet
Coming from the village street
Just beyond the parson's wall,
Where the clover globes are sweet
And the mushroom's parasol
Opens in the moonlit rain.
Every night I hear them call
From their long and merry train.
Old lame Bridget says to me,
"It is just your fancy, child."
She cannot believe I see
Laughing faces in the wild,
Hands that twinkle in the sedge
Bowing at the water's edge
Where the finny minnows quiver,
Shaping on a blue wave's ledge
Bubble foam to sail the river.
And the sunny hands to me
Beckon ever, beckon ever.
Oh! I would be wild and free,
And with the shadow people be.

In A Cafe

Kiss the maid and pass her round,
Lips like hers were made for many.
Our loves are far from us to-night,
But these red lips are sweet as any.

Let no empty glass be seen
Aloof from our good table's sparkle,
At the acme of our cheer
Here are francs to keep the circle.

They are far who miss us most-
Sip and kiss -how well we love them,
Battling through the world to keep
Their hearts at peace, their God above them.

The Lost Ones

Somewhere is music from the linnets' bills,
And thro' the sunny flowers the bee-wings drone,
And white bells of convolvulus on hills

Of quiet May make silent ringing, blown
Hither and thither by the wind of showers,
And somewhere all the wandering birds have flown;
And the brown breath of Autumn chills the flowers.

But where are all the loves of long ago?
O little twilight ship blown up the tide,
Where are the faces laughing in the glow
Of morning years, the lost ones scattered wide
Give me your hand, O brother, let us go
Crying about the dark for those who died.

With Flowers

These have more language than my song,
Take them and let them speak for me.
I whispered them a secret thing
Down the green lanes of Allary.

You shall remember quiet ways
Watching them fade, and quiet eyes,
And two hearts given up to love,
A foolish and an overwise.

After Court Martial

My mind is not my mind, therefore
I take no heed of what men say,
I lived ten thousand years before
God cursed the town of Nineveh.

The Present is a dream I see
Of horror and loud sufferings,
At dawn a bird will waken me
Unto my place among the kings.

And though men called me a vile name,
And all my dream companions gone,
Tis I the soldier bears the shame,
Not I the king of Babylon.

The Lanawn Shee

Powdered and perfumed the full bee
Winged heavily across the clover,

And where the hills were dim with dew,
Purple and blue the west leaned over.

A willow spray dipped in the stream,
Moving a gleam of silver ringing,
And by a finny creek a maid
Filled all the shade with softest singing.

Listening, my heart and soul at strife,
On the edge of life I seemed to hover,'
For I knew my love had come at last,
That my joy was past and my gladness over.

I tiptoed gently up and stooped
Above her looped and shining tresses,
And asked her of her kin and name,
And why she came from fairy places.

She told me of a sunny coast
Beyond the most adventurous sailor,
Where she had spent a thousand years
Out of the fears that now assail her.

And there, she told me, honey drops
Out of the tops of ash and willow,
And in the mellow shadow Sleep
Doth sweetly keep her poppy pillow.

Nor Autumn with her brown line marks
The time of larks, the length of roses,
But song-time there is over never
Nor flower-time ever, ever closes.

And wildly through uncurling ferns
Fast water turns down valleys singing,
Filling with scented winds the dales,
Setting the bells of sleep a-ringing.

And when the thin moon lowly sinks,'
Through cloudy chinks a silver glory
Lingers upon the left of night
Till dawn delights the meadows hoary.

And by the lakes the skies are white,
(Oh, the delight!) when swans are coming,
Among the flowers sweet joy-bells peal,
And quick bees wheel in drowsy humming

The squirrel leaves her dusty house
And in the boughs makes fearless gambol,
And, falling down in fire-drops, red,
The fruit is shed from every bramble.

Then, gathered all about the trees
Glad galaxies of youth are dancing,
Treading the perfume of the flowers,
Filling the hours with mazy glancing.

And when the dance is done, the trees
Are left to Peace and the brown woodpecker,
And on the western slopes of sky
The day's blue eye begins to flicker.

But at the sighing of the leaves,
When all earth grieves for lights departed
An ancient and a sad desire
Steals in to tire the human-hearted.

No fairy aid can save them now
Nor turn their prow upon the ocean,
The hundred years that missed each heart
Above them start their wheels in motion.

And so our loves are lost, she sighed,
And far and wide we seek new treasure,
For who on Time or Timeless hills
Can live the ills of loveless leisure?

(' Fairer than Usna's youngest son,
0, my poor one, what flower-bed holds you?
Or, wrecked upon the shores of home,
What wave of foam with white enfolds you?

' You rode with kings on hills of green,
And lovely queens have served you banquet,
Sweet wine from berries bruised they brought
And shyly sought the lips which drank it.

' But in your dim grave of the sea
There shall not be a friend to love you.
And ever heedless of your loss
The earth ships cross the storms above you.

' And still the chase goes on, and still

The wine shall spill, and vacant places
Be given over to the new
As love untrue keeps changing faces.

' And I must wander with my song
Far from the young till Love returning,
Brings me the beautiful reward
Of some heart stirred by my long yearning.')

Friend, have you heard a bird lament
When sleet is sent for April weather?
As beautiful she told her grief,
As down through leaf and flower I led her.

And friend, could I remain unstirred
Without a word for such a sorrow?
Say, can the lark forget the cloud
When poppies shroud the seeded furrow?

Like a poor widow whose late grief
Seeks for relief in lonely byeways,
The moon, companionless and dim,
Took her dull rim through starless highways.

I was too weak with dreams to feel
Enchantment steal with guilt upon me,
She slipped, a flower upon the wind,
And laughed to find how she had won me.

From hill to hill, from land to land,
Her lovely hand is beckoning for me,
I follow on through dangerous zones,
Cross dead men's bones and oceans stormy.

Some day I know she'll wait at last
And lock me fast in white embraces,
And down mysterious ways of love
We two shall move to fairy places.

Youth
She paved the way with perfume sweet
Of flowers that moved like winds alight,
And never weary grew my feet
Wandering through[the spring's delight.

She dropped her sweet fife to her lips
And lured me with her melodies,
To where the great big wandering ships
Put out into the peaceful seas.

But when the year grew chill and brown,
And all the wings of Summer flown,
Within the tumult of a town
She left me to grow old alone.

The Dead Kings
All the dead kings came to me
At Rosnaree, where I was dreaming.
A few stars glimmered through the morn,
And down the thorn the dews were streaming.

And every dead king had a story
Of ancient glory, sweetly told.
It was too early for the lark,
But the starry dark had tints of gold.

I listened to the sorrows three
Of that Eire passed into song.
A cock crowed near a hazel croft,
And up aloft dim larks winged strong.

And I, too, told the kings a story
Of later glory, her fourth sorrow:
There was a sound like moving shields
In high green fields and the lowland furrow.

And one said: ' We who yet are kings
Have heard these things lamenting inly.'
Sweet music flowed from many a bill
And on the hill the morn stood queenly.

And one said: ' Over is the singing,
And bell bough ringing, whence we come;
With heavy hearts we'll tread the shadows,
In honey meadows birds are dumb.'

And one said: ' Since the poets perished
And all they cherished in the way,
Their thoughts unsung, like petal showers
Inflame the hours of blue and gray.'

And one said: ' A loud tramp of men
We'll hear again at Rosnaree.'
A bomb burst near me where I lay.
I woke, 'twas day in Picardy.

The Little Children
Hunger points a bony finger
To the workhouse on the hill,
But the little children linger
While there's flowers to gather still
For my sunny window sill.

In my hands I take their faces,
Smiling to my smiles they run.
Would that I could take their places
Where the murky bye-ways shun
The benedictions of the sun

How they laugh and sing returning
Lightly on their secret way.
While I listen in my yearning
Their laughter fills the windy day
With gladness, youth and May.

Spring Love
I saw her coming through the flowery grass,
Round her swift ankles butterfly and bee
Blent loud and silent wings ; I saw her pass
Where foam-bows shivered on the sunny sea.

Then came the swallow crowding up the dawn,
And cuckoo-echoes filled the dewy South.
I left my love upon the hill, alone,
My last kiss burning on her lovely mouth.

Spring And Autumn
Green ripples singing down the corn,
With blossoms dumb the path I tread,
And in the music of the morn
One with wild roses on her head.

Now the green ripples turn to gold
And all the paths are loud with rain,
I with desire am growing old
And full of winter pain.

Spring
Once more the lark with song and speed
Cleaves through the dawn, his hurried bars;
Fall, like the flute of Ganymede
Twirling and whistling from the stars.

The primrose and the daffodil
Surprise the valleys, and wild thyme
Is sweet on every little hill,
When lambs come down at folding time.

In every wild place now is heard
The magpie's noisy house, and through
The mingled tunes of many a bird
The ruffled wood-dove's gentle coo.

Sweet by the river's noisy brink
The water-lily bursts her crown,
The kingfisher comes down to drink
Like rainbow jewels falling down.

And when the blue and grey entwine
The daisy shuts her golden eye,
And peace wraps all those hills of mine
Safe in my dearest memory.

June
Broom out the floor now, lay the fender by,
And plant this bee-sucked bough of woodbine there,
And let the window down. The butterfly
Floats in upon the sunbeam, and the fair
Tanned face of June, the nomad gipsy, laughs
Above her widespread wares, the while she tells
The farmers' fortunes in the fields, and quaffs
The water from the spider-peopled wells.
The hedges are all drowned in green grass seas,
And bobbing poppies flare like Elmo's light,

While siren-like the pollen-staind bees
Drone in the clover depths. And up the height
The cuckoo's voice is hoarse and broke with joy.
And on the lowland crops the crows make raid,
Nor fear the clappers of the farmer's boy,
Who sleeps, like drunken Noah, in the shad
And loop this red rose in that hazel ring
That snares your little ear, for June is short
And we must joy in it and dance and sing,
And from her bounty draw her rosy worth.
Ay! soon the swallows will be flying south,
The wind wheel north to gather in the snow,
Even the roses spilt on youth's red mouth
Will soon blow down the road all roses go.

Autumn
Now leafy winds are blowing cold,
And South by West the sun goes down,
A quiet huddles up the fold
In sheltered corners of the brown.

Like scattered fire the wild fruit strews
The ground beneath the blowing tree,
And there the busy squirrel hews
His deep and secret granary.

And when the night comes starry clear,
The lonely quail complains beside
The glistening waters on the mere
Where widowed Beauties yet abide.

And I, too, make my own complaint
Upon a reed I plucked in June,
And love to hear it echoed faint
Upon another heart in tune.

A Mother's Song
Little ships of whitest pearl
With sailors who were ancient kings,
Come over the sea when my little girl
Sings.

And if my little girl should weep,

Little ships with torn sails
Go headlong down among the deep
Whales.

A Rainy Day in April

When the clouds shake their hyssops, and the rain
Like holy water falls upon the plain,
'Tis sweet to gaze upon the springing grain
And see your harvest born.

And sweet the little breeze of melody
The blackbord puffs upon teh budding tree,
While the wild poppy lights upon the lea
And blazes 'mid the corn.

The skylark soars the freshening shower to hail,
And the meek daisy holds aloft her pail.
And Spring all radiant by the wayside pale
Sets up her rock and reel.

See how she weaves her mantle fold on fold,
Hemming the woods and carpeting the wold.
Her warp is of the green, her woof the gold,
The spinning world her wheel.

The Call To Ireland

We have fought so much for the nation
In the tents we helped to divide;
Shall the cause of our common fathers
On our earthstones lie denied?
For the price of a field we have wrangled
While the weather rusted the plow,
' twas yours and 'twas mine and 'tis ours yet
And it's time to be fencing it now.

Ardan Mór

As I was climbing Ardan Mór
From the shore of Sheelin lake,
I met the herons coming down
Before the water's wake.

And they were talking in their flight
Of dreamy ways the herons go
When all the hills are withered up
Nor any waters flow.

To My Best Friend
I love the wet-lipped wind that stirs the hedge
And kisses the bent flowers that drooped for rain,
That stirs the poppy on the sun-burned ledge
And like a swan dies singing, without pain.
The golden bees go buzzing down to stain
The lilies' frills, and the blue harebell rings,
And the sweet blackbird in the rainbow sings.

Deep in the meadows I would sing a song,
The shallow brook my tuning-fork, the birds
My masters; and the boughs they hop along
Shall mark my time: but there shall be no words
For lurking Echo's mock; an angel herds
Words that I may not know, within, for you,
Words for the faithful meet, the good and true.

Bound To The Mast
When mildly falls the deluge of the grass,
And meads begin to rise like Noah's flood,
And o'er the hedgerows flow, and onward pass,
Dribbling thro' many a wood:
When hawthorn trees their flags of truce unfurl,
And dykes are spitting violets to the breeze;
When meadow larks their jocund flight will curl
From Earth's to Heaven's leas;
Ah! then the poet's dreams are most sublime,
A-sail on seas that know a heavenly calm,
And in his song you hear the river's rhyme,
And the first bleat of the lamb.
Then when the summer evenings fall serene,
Unto the country dance his songs repair,
And you may meet some maids with angel mien,
Bright eyes and twilight hair.
When Autumn's crayon tones the green leaves sere,
And breezes honed on icebergs hurry past;
When meadow-tides have ebbed and woods grow drear,
And bow before the blast;

When briars make semicircles on the way;
When blackbirds hide their flutes and cower and die;
When swollen rivers lose themselves and stray
Beneath a murky sky;
Then doth the poet's voice like cuckoo's break,
And round his verse the hungry lapwing grieves,
And melancholy in his dreary wake
The funeral of the leaves.
Then when the Autumn dies upon the plain,
Wound in the snow alike his right and wrong,
The poet sings, albeit a sad strain,
Bound to the Mast of Song.

A Rainy Day In April
When the clouds shake their hyssops, and the rain
Like holy water falls upon the plain,
Tis sweet to gaze upon the springing grain
And see your harvest born.

And sweet the little breeze of melody,
The blackbird puffs upon the budding tree,
While the wild poppy lights upon the lea
And blazes 'mid the corn.

The skylark soars the freshening shower to hail,
And the meek daisy holds aloft her pail,
And Spring all radiant by the wayside pale,
Sets up her rock and reel.

See how she weaves her mantle fold on fold,
Hemming the woods and carpeting the wold.
Her warp is of the green, her woof the gold,
The spinning world her wheel.

By'n by above the hills a pilgrim moon
Will rise to light upon the midnight noon,
But still she plieth to the lonesome tune
Of the brown meadow rail.

No heavy dreams upon her eyelids weigh,
Nor do her busy fingers ever stay ;
She knows a fairy prince is on the way
To wake a sleeping beauty.

To deck the pathway that his feet must tread,

To fringe the 'broidery of the roses' bed,
To show the Summer she but sleeps, not dead,
This is her fixed duty.

ENVOI
To-day while leaving my dear home behind,
My eyes with salty homesick teardrops blind,
The rain fell on me sorrowful and kind
Like angels' tears of pity.

Twas then I heard the small birds' melodies,
And saw the poppies' bonfire on the leas,
As Spring came whispering thro' the leafing trees
Giving to me my ditty.

A Song Of April
The censer of the eglantine was moved
By little lane winds, and the watching faces
Of garden flowerets, which of old she loved,
Peep shyly outward from their silent places.

But when the sun arose the flowers grew bolder,
And she will be in white, I thought, and she
Will have a cuckoo on her either shoulder,
And woodbine twines and fragrant wings of pea.

And I will meet her on the hills of South,
And I will lead her to a northern water,
My wild one, the sweet beautiful uncouth,
The eldest maiden of the Winter's daughter.

And down the rainbows of her noon shall slide
Lark music, and the little sunbeam people,
And nomad wings shall fill the river side,
And ground winds rocking in the lily's steeple.

Waiting
A strange old woman on the wayside sate,
Looked far away and shook her head and sighed.
And when anon, close by, a rusty gate
Loud on the warm winds cried,
She lifted up her eyes and said, "You're late."
Then shook her head and sighed.

And evening found her thus, and night in state
Walked thro' the starlight, and a heavy tide
Followed the yellow moon around her wait,
And morning walked in wide.
She lifted up her eyes and said, "You're late."
Then shook her head and sighed.

The Singer's Muse
I brought in these to make her kitchen sweet,
Haw blossoms and the roses of the lane.
Her heart seemed in her eyes so wild they beat
With welcome for the boughs of Spring again.

She never heard of Babylon or Troy,
She read no book, but once saw Dublin town;
Yet she made a poet of her servant boy
And from Parnassus earned the laurel crown.

If Fame, the Gorgon, turns me into stone
Upon some city square, let someone place
Thorn blossoms and lane roses newly blown
Beside my feet, and underneath them trace:

"His heart was like a bookful of girls' song,
With little loves and mighty Care's alloy.
These did he bring his muse, and suffered long,
Her bashful singer and her servant boy."

Inamorata
The bees were holding levees in the flowers,
Do you remember how each puff of wind
Made every wing a hum? My hand in yours
Was listening to your heart, but now
The glory is all faded, and I find
No more the olden mystery of the hours
When you were lovely and our hearts would bow

Each to the will of each, but one bright day
Is stretching like an isthmus in a bay
From the glad years that I have left behind.
I look across the edge of things that were
And you are lovely in the April ways,

Holy and mute, the sigh of my despair. . . .

I hear once more the linnets' April tune
Beyond the rainbow's warp, as in the days
You brought me facefuls of your smiles to share
Some of your new-found wonders. . . . Oh when soon
I'm wandering the wide seas for other lands,
Sometimes remember me with folded hands,
And keep me happy in your pious prayer.

The Hills

The hills are crying from the fields to me,
And calling me with music from a choir
Of waters in their woods where I can see
The bloom unfolded on the whins like fire.
And, as the evening moon climbs ever higher
And blots away the shadows from the slope,
They cry to me like things devoid of hope.

Pigeons are home. Day droops. The fields are cold.
Now a slow wind comes labouring up the sky
With a small cloud long steeped in sunset gold,
Like Jason with the precious fleece anigh
The harbour of Iolcos. Day's bright eye
Is filmed with the twilight, and the rill
Shines like a scimitar upon the hill.

And moonbeams drooping thro' the coloured wood
Are full of little people winged white.
I'll wander thro' the moon-pale solitude
That calls across the intervening night
With river voices at their utmost height,
Sweet as rain-water in the blackbird's flute
That strikes the world in admiration mute.

In Manchester

There is a noise of feet that move in sin
Under the side-faced moon here where I stray,
Want by me like a Nemesis. The din
Of noon is in my ears, but far away
My thoughts are, where Peace shuts the black-birds' wings
And it is cherry time by all the springs.

And this same moon floats like a trail of fire
Down the long Boyne, and darts white arrows thro'
The mill wood; her white skirt is on the weir,
She walks thro' crystal mazes of the dew,
And rests awhile upon the dewy slope
Where I will hope again the old, old hope.

With wandering we are worn my muse and I,
And, if I sing, my song knows nought of mirth.
I often think my soul is an old lie
In sackcloth, it repents so much of birth.
But I will build it yet a cloister home
Near the peace of lakes when I have ceased to roam.

Music On Water
Where does Remembrance weep when we forget?
From whither brings she back an old delight?
Why do we weep that once we laughed? and yet
Why are we sad that once our hearts were light?
I sometimes think the days that we made bright
Are damned within us, and we hear them yell,
Deep in the solitude of that wide hell,
Because we welcome in some new regret.

I will remember with sad heart next year
This music and this water, but to-day
Let me be part of all this joy. My ear
Caught far-off music which I bid away,
The light of one fair face that fain would stay
Upon the heart's broad canvas, as the Face
On Mary's towel, lighting up the place.
Too sad for joy, too happy for a tear.

Methinks I see the music like a light
Low on the bobbing water, and the fields
Yellow and brown alternate on the height,
Hanging in silence there like battered shields,
Lean forward heavy with their coloured yields
As if they paid it homage; and the strains,
Prisoners of Echo, up the sunburnt plains
Fade on the cross-cut to a future night.

In the red West the twisted moon is low,
And on the bubbles there are half-lit stars:
Music and twilight: and the deep blue flow

Of water: and the watching fire of Mars:
The deep fish slipping thro' the moonlit bars
Make Death a thing of sweet dreams, life a mock.
And the soul patient by the heart's loud clock
Watches the time, and thinks it wondrous slow.

The Visitation Of Peace

I closed the book of verse where Sorrow wept
Above Love's broken fane where Hope once prayed,
And thought of old trysts broken and trysts kept
Only to chide my fondness. Then I strayed

Down a green coil of lanes where murmuring wings
Moved up and down like lights upon the sea,
Searching for calm amid untroubled things
Of wood and water. The industrious bee
Sang in his barn within the hollow beech,
And in a distant haggard a loud mill
Hummed like a war of hives. A whispered speech
Of corn and wind was on the yellow hill,
And tattered scarecrows nodded their assent
And waved their arms like orators. The brown
Nude beauty of the Autumn sweetly bent
Over the woods, across the little town.
I sat in a retreating shade beside
The river, where it fell across a weir
Like a white mane, and in a flourish wide
Roars by an island field and thro' a tier
Of leaning sallies, like an avenue
When the moon's flambeau hunts the shadows out
And strikes the borders white across the dew.
Where little ringlets ended, the fleet trout
Fed on the water moths. A marsh hen crossed
On flying wings and swimming feet to where
Her mate was in the rushes forest, tossed
On the heaving dusk like swallows in the air.

Beyond the river a walled rood of graves
Hung dead with all its hemlock wan and sere,
Save where the wall was broken and long waves
Of yellow grass flowed outward like a weir,
As if the dead were striving for more room
And their old places in the scheme of things;
For sometimes the thought comes that the brown tomb
Is not the end of all our labourings,

But we are born once more of wind and rain,
To sow the world with harvest young and strong,
That men may live by men 'til the stars wane,
And still sweet music fill the blackbird's song.

But O for truths about the soul denied.
Shall I meet Keats in some wild isle of balm,
Dreaming beside a tarn where green and wide
Boughs of sweet cinnamon protect the calm
Of the dark water? And together walk
Thro' hills with dimples full of water where
White angels rest, and all the dead years talk
About the changes of the earth? Despair
Sometimes takes hold of me but yet I hope
To hope the old hope in the better times
When I am free to cast aside the rope
That binds me to all sadness 'til my rhymes
Cry like lost birds. But O, if I should die
Ere this millennium, and my hands be crossed
Under the flowers I loved, the passers-by
Shall scowl at me as one whose soul is lost.
But a soft peace came to me when the West
Shut its red door and a thin streak of moon
Was twisted on the twilight's dusky breast.

It wrapped me up as sometimes a sweet tune
Heard for the first time wraps the scenes around,
That we may have their memories when some hand
Strikes it in other times and hopes unbound
Rising see clear the everlasting land.

Before The Tears
You looked as sad as an eclipsed moon
Above the sheaves of harvest, and there lay
A light lisp on your tongue, and very soon
The petals of your deep blush fell away;
White smiles that come with an uneasy grace
From inner sorrow crossed your forehead fair,
When the wind passing took your scattered hair
And flung it like a brown shower in my face.

Tear- fringed winds that fill the heart's low sighs
And never break upon the bosom's pain,
But blow unto the windows of the eyes
Their misty promises of silver rain,

Around your loud heart ever rose and fell.
I thought 'twere better that the tears should come
And strike your every feeling wholly numb,
So thrust my hand in yours and shook farewell.

God's Rememberance

There came a whisper from the night to me
Like music of the sea, a mighty breath
From out the valley's dewy mouth, and Death
Shook his lean bones, and every coloured tree
Wept in the fog of morning. From the town
Of nests among the branches one old crow
With gaps upon his wings flew far away.
And, thinking of the golden summer glow,
I heard a blackbird whistle half his lay
Among the spinning leaves that slanted down.

And I who am a thought of God's now long
Forgotten in His Mind, and desolate
With other dreams long over, as a gate
Singing upon the wind the anvil song,
Sang of the Spring when first He dreamt of me
In that old town all hills and signs that creak:
And He remembered me as something far
In old imaginations, something weak
With distance, like a little sparking star
Drowned in the lavender of evening sea.

A Memory

Sounds of night that drip upon the ear,
The plumed lapwing's cry, the curlew's call,
Clear in the far dark heard, a sound as drear
As raindrops pelted from a nodding rush
To give a white wink once and broken fall
Into a deep dark pool: they pain the hush,
As if the fiery meteor's slanting lance
Had found their empty craws: they fill with sound
The silence, with the merry round,
The sounding mazes of a last year's dance.

I thought to watch the stars come spark by spark
Out on the muffled night, and watch the moon
Go round the full, and turn upon the dark,

And sharpen towards the new, and waiting watch
The grand Kaleidoscope of midnight noon
Change colours on the dew, where high hills notch
The low and moony sky. But who dare cast
One brief hour's horoscope, whose tuned ear
Makes every sound the music of last year?
Whose hopes are built up in the door of Past?

No, not more silent does the spider stitch
A cobweb on the fern, nor fogdrops fall
On sheaves of harvest when the night is rich
With moonbeams, than the spirits of delight
Walk the dark passages of Memory's hall.
We feel them not, but in the wastes of night
We hear their low-voiced mediums, and we rise
To wrestle old Regrets, to see old faces,
To meet and part in old tryst-trodden places
With breaking heart, and emptying of eyes.

I feel the warm hand on my shoulder light,
I hear the music of a voice that words
The slow time of the feet, I see the white
Arms slanting, and the dimples fold and fill. . . .
I hear wing-flutters of the early birds,
I see the tide of morning landward spill,
The cloaking maidens, hear the voice that tells
"You'd never know" and " Soon perhaps again?'
With white teeth biting down the inly pain,
Then sounds of going away and "sad farewells.

A year ago! It seems but yesterday.
Yesterday! And a hundred years! All one.
'Tis laid a something finished, dark, away,
To gather mould upon the shelves of Time.
What matters - hours or aeons when 'tis gone?
And yet the heart will dust it of its grime,
And hover round it in a silver spell,
Be lost in it and cry aloud in fear;
And like a lost soul in a pious ear,
Hammer in mine a never easy bell.

A Fear
I roamed the woods to-day and seemed to hear,
As Dante heard, the voice of suffering trees.
The twisted roots seemed bare contorted knees,

The bark was full of faces strange with fear.

I hurried home still wrapt in that dark spell,
And all the night upon the world's great lie
I pondered, and a voice seemed whisp'ring nigh,
"You died long since, and all this thing is hell!"

The Coming Poet
"Is it far to the town?" said the poet,
As he stood 'neath the groaning vane,
And the warm lights shimmered silver
On the skirts of the windy rain.

"There are those who call me," he pleaded,
"And I'm wet and travel sore."
But nobody spoke from the shelter,
And he turned from the bolted door.

And they wait in the town for the poet
With stones at the gates, and jeers,
But away on the wolds of distance
In the blue of a thousand years

He sleeps with the age that knows him,
In the clay of the unborn, dead,
Rest at his weary insteps,
Fame at his crumbled head.

The Vision On The Brink
Tonight when you sit in the deep hours alone,
And from the sleeps you snatch wake quick and feel
You hear my step upon the threshold-stone,

My hand upon the doorway latchward steal,
Be sure 'tis but the white winds of the snow,
For I shall come no more.

And when the candle in the pane is wore,
And moonbeams down the hill long shadows throw,
When night's white eyes are in the chinky door,

Think of a long road in a valley low,
Think of a wanderer in the distance far,

Lost like a voice among the scattered hills.

And when the moon has gone and ocean spills
Its waters backward from the trysting bar,
And in dark furrows of the night there tills

A jewelled plough, and many a falling star
Moves you to prayer, then will you think of me
On the long road that will not ever end.

Jonah is hoarse in Nineveh I'd lend
My voice to save the town and hurriedly
Goes Abraham with murdering knife, and Ruth

Is weary in the corn. . . . Yet will I stay,
For one flower blooms upon the rocks of truth,
God is in all our hurry and delay.

The Sister
I saw the little quiet town,
And the whitewashed gables on the hill,
And laughing children coming down
The laneway to the mill.

Wind-blushes up their faces glowed,
And they were happy as could be,
The wobbling water never flowed
So merry and so free.

One little maid withdrew aside
To pick a pebble from the sands.
Her golden hair was long and wide,
And there were dimples on her hands.

And when I saw her large blue eyes,
What was the pain that went thro' me?
Why did I think on Southern skies
And ships upon the sea?

Low Moon Land
I often look when the moon is low
Thro' that other window on the wall,
At a land all beautiful under snow,

Blotted with shadows that come and go
When the winds rise up and fall.
And the form of a beautiful maid
In the white silence stands,
And beckons me with her hands.

And when the cares of the day are laid,
Like sacred things, in the mart away,
I dream of the low-moon land and the maid
Who will not weary of waiting, or jade
Of calling to me for aye.
And I would go if I knew the sea
That lips the shore where the moon is low,
For a longing is on me that will not go.

On Dream Water
And so, o'er many a league of sea
We sang of those we left behind.
Our ship split thro' the phosphor free,
Her white sails pregnant with the wind,
And I was wondering in my mind
How many would remember me.

Then red-edged dawn expanded wide,
A stony foreland stretched away,
And bowed capes gathering round the tide
Kept many a little homely bay.
O joy of living there for aye,
O Soul so often tried!

Growing Old
We'll fill a Provence bowl and. pledge us deep
The memory of the far ones, and between
The soothing pipes, in heavy-lidded sleep,
Perhaps we'll dream the things that once have been.

Tis only noon and still too soon to die,
Yet we are growing old, my heart and I.
A hundred books are ready in my head
To open out where Beauty bent a leaf.

What do we want with Beauty? We are wed
Like ancient Proserpine to dismal grief.

And we are changing with the hours that fly,
And growing odd and old, my heart and I.

Across a bed of bells the river flows,
And roses dawn, but not for us; we want
The new thing ever as the old thing grows
Spectral and weary on the hills we haunt.
And that is why we feast, and that is why
We're growing odd and old, my heart and I.

After My Last Song
Where I shall rest when my last song is over
The air is smelling like a feast of wine;
And purple breakers of the windy clover
Shall roll to cool this burning brow of mine;
And there shall come to me, when day is told
The peace of sleep when I am grey and old.

I'm wild for wandering to the far-off places
Since one forsook me whom I held most dear.
I want to see new wonders and new faces
Beyond East seas ; but I will win back here
When my last song is sung, and veins are cold
As thawing snow, and I am grey and old.

Oh paining eyes, but not with salty weeping,
My heart is like a sod in winter rain;
Ere you will see those baying waters leaping
Like hungry hounds once more, how many a pain
Shall heal; but when my last short song is trolled
You'll sleep here on wan cheeks grown thin and old.

To A Distant One
Through wild by-ways I come to you, my love,
Nor ask of those I meet the surest way,
What way I turn I cannot go astray
And miss you in my life. Though Fate may prove

A tardy guide she will not make delay
Leading me through strange seas and distant lands,
I'm coming still, though slowly, to your hands.
We'll meet one day.
There is so much to do, so little done,

In my life's space that I perforce did leave
Love at the moonlit trysting-place to grieve

Till fame and other little things were won.
I have missed much that I shall not retrieve,
Far will I wander yet with much to do.
Much will I spurn before I yet meet you,
So fair I can't deceive.

Your name is in the whisper of the woods
Like Beauty calling for a poet's song
To one whose harp had suffered many a wrong
In the lean hands of Pain. And when the broods

Of flower eyes waken all the streams along
In tender whiles, I feel most near to you:
Oh, when we meet there shall be sun and blue
Strong as the spring is strong.

Evening In England
From its blue vase the rose of evening drops.
Upon the streams its petals float away.
The hills all blue with distance hide their tops
In the dim silence falling on the grey.

A little wind said "Hush!" and shook a spray
Heavy with May's white crop of opening bloom,
A silent bat went dipping up the gloom.

Night tells her rosary of stars full soon,
They drop from out her dark hand to her knees.

Upon a silhouette of woods the moon
Leans on one horn as if beseeching ease
From all her changes which have stirred the seas.

Across the ears of Toil Rest throws her veil,
I and a marsh bird only make a wail.

In The Mediterranean Going To The War
Lovely wings of gold and green
Flit about the sounds I hear,
On my window when I lean

To the shadows cool and clear.

Roaming, I am listening still,
Bending, listening overlong,
In my soul a steadier will,
In my heart a newer song.

Autumn Evening In Serbia

All the thin shadows
Have closed on the grass,
With the drone on their dark wings
The night beetles pass.

Folded her eyelids,
A maiden asleep,
Day sees in her chamber
The pallid moon peep.

From the bend of the briar
The roses are torn.
And the folds of the wood tops
Are faded and worn.

A strange bird is singing
Sweet notes of the sun,
Tho' song time is over
And Autumn begun.

Nocturne

The rim of the moon
Is over the corn.
The beetle's drone
Is above the thorn.

Grey days come soon
And I am alone;
Can you hear my moan
Where you rest, Aroon?

When the wild tree bore
The deep blue cherry,
In night's deep hall
Our love kissed merry.

But you come no more
Where its woodlands call,
And the grey days fall
On my grief, Astore!

When Love And Beauty Wander Away
When Love and Beauty wander away,
And there's no more hearts to be sought and won,
When the old earth limps thro' the dreary day,
And the work of the Seasons cry undone:
Ah! what shall we do for a song to sing,
Who have known Beauty, and Love, and Spring?

When Love and Beauty wander away,
And a pale fear lies on the cheeks of youth,
When there's no more goal to strive for and pray,
And we live at the end of the world's untruth:
Ah! what shall we do for a heart to prove,
Who have known Beauty, and Spring, and Love?

The Resurrection
My true love still is all that's fair,
She is flower and blossom blowing free,
For all her silence lying there
She sings a spirit song to me.

New lovers seek her in her bower,
The rain, the dew, the flying wind,
And tempt her out to be a flower,
Which throws a shadow on my mind.

The Ships Of Arcady
Thro' the faintest filigree
Over the dim waters go
Little ships of Arcady
When the morning moon is low.

I can hear the sailors' song
From the blue edge of the sea,
Passing like the lights along

Thro' the dusky filigree.

Then where moon and waters meet
Sail by sail they pass away,
With little friendly winds replete
Blowing from the breaking day.

And when the little ships have flown,
Dreaming still of Arcady
I look across the waves, alone
In the misty filigree.

An Attempt At A City Sunset
There was a quiet glory in the sky
When thro' the gables sank the large red sun,
And toppling mounts of rugged cloud went by
Heavy with whiteness, and the moon had won
Her way above the woods, with her small star
Behind her like the cuckoo's little mother. . . .
It was the hour when visions from some far
Strange Eastern dreams like twilight bats take
wing
Out of the ruin of memories.

O brother

Of high song, wand'ring where the Muses fling
si

Rich gifts as prodigal as winter rain,
Like stepping-stones within a swollen river
The hidden words are sounding in my brain,
Too wild for taming ; and I must for ever
Think of the hills upon the wilderness,
And leave the city sunset to your song.
For there I am a stranger like the trees
That sigh upon the traffic all day long.

Before The War Of Cooley
At daybreak Maeve rose up from where she prayed
And took her prophetess across her door
To gaze upon her hosts. Tall spear and blade
Burnished for early battle dimly shook
The morning's colours, and then Maeve said :

"Look
And tell me how you see them now."
And then
The woman that was lean with knowledge said :
"There's crimson on them, and there's dripping red."

And a tall soldier galloped up the glen no

BEFORE THE WAR OF COOLEY in
With foam upon his boot, and halted there
Beside old Maeve. She said, " Not yet," and
turned

Into her blazing dun, and knelt in prayer
One solemn hour, and once again she came
And sought her prophetess. With voice that

mourned,
" How do you see them now ? " she asked.

" All lame

And broken in the noon." And once again
The soldier stood before her.

" No, not yet."

Maeve answered his inquiring look and turned
Once more unto her prayer, and yet once more
" How do you see them now ? " she asked.

" All wet
With storm rains, and all broken, and all tore

With midnight wolves." And when the

soldier came
Maeve said, " It is the hour." There was a

flash

Of trumpets in the dim, a silver flame
Of rising shields, loud words passed down the

ranks,

And twenty feet they saw the lances leap.
They passed the dun with one short noisy dash.
And turning proud Maeve gave the wise one

thanks,
And sought her chamber in the dun to weep.

The Death Of Sualtem
After the brown bull passed from Cooley's
fields

And all Muirevne was a wail of pain,
Sualtem came at evening thro' the slain
And heard a noise like water rushing loud,
A thunder like the noise of mighty shields.
And in his dread he shouted : " Earth is bowed,
The heavens are split and stars make war with
stars
And the sea runs in fear ! "

For all his scars
He hastened to Dun Dealgan, and there found
It was his son, Curculain, making moan.
His hair was red with blood and he was wound
In wicker full of grass, and a cold stone
Was on his head.

" Cuculain, is it so ? "

Sualtem said, and then, " My hair is snow,
My strength leaks thro' my wounds, but I will

die
Avenging you/'

And then Cuculain said :
" Not so, old father, but take horse and ride
To Emain Macha, and tell Connor this."

Sualtem from his red lips took a kiss,
And turned the stone upon Cuculain's head.
The Lia-Macha with a heavy sigh
Ran up and halted by his wounded side.

In Emain Macha to low lights and song
Connor was dreaming of the beauteous Maeve.
He saw her as at first, by Shannon's wave,
Her insteps in the water, mounds of white.
It was in Spring, and music loud and strong
Rocked all the coloured woods, and the blue
height

Of heaven was round the lark, and in his heart
There was a pain of love.

Then with a start
He wakened as a loud voice from below
Shouted, " The land is robbed, the women
shamed,

The children stolen, and Curculain low! "
Then Connor rose, his war-worn soul inflamed,
And shouted down for Cathbad; then to greet
The messenger he hurried to the street.

And there he saw Sualtem shouting still
The message of Muirevne 'mid the sound
Of hurried bucklings and uneasy horse.
At sight of him the Lia-Macha wheeled,
So that Sualtem fell upon his shield,
And his grey head came shouting to the
ground.

They buried him by moonlight on the hill,
And all about him waves the heavy gorse.

Printed in Great Britain
by Amazon